I Can Do It!

I Can Clean Up

By Meg Gaertner

level 1 little blue readers

www.littlebluehousebooks.com

Little Blue House is distributed by North Star Editions
sales@northstareditions.com | 888-417-0195

Produced for Little Blue House by Red Line Editorial.

Photographs ©: Shutterstock Images cover, 7, 11, 12–13, 16–17, 19, 23, 24 (top right), 24 (bottom left), 24 (bottom right); iStockphoto, 4, 8–9, 15, 20–21, 24 (top left)

Library of Congress Control Number: 2022901673

ISBN
978-1-64619-577-0 (hardcover)
978-1-64619-604-3 (paperback)
978-1-64619-657-9 (ebook pdf)
978-1-64619-631-9 (hosted ebook)

Printed in the United States of America
Mankato, MN
082022

About the Author

Meg Gaertner enjoys reading, writing, dancing, and being outside. She lives in Minnesota.

Table of Contents

I Can Clean Up **5**

Glossary **24**

Index **24**

bed
MERRY CHRISTMAS

I Can Clean Up

I clean up in the bedroom.

I make my bed.

I clean up in
the bedroom.
I put away my toys.

toy

I clean up in

the bedroom.

I fold my clothes.

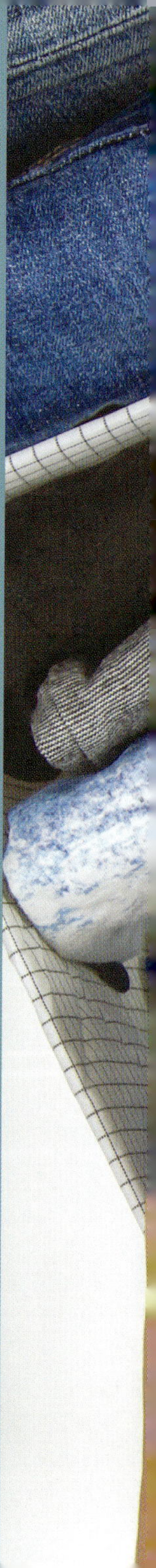

clothes

I clean up in the
dining room.
I wipe up my spills.

spill

I clean up in the
dining room.
I clear the table.

table

I clean up in the kitchen.

I dry the dishes.

dish

I clean up in the kitchen.

I put away the plates.

plate

I clean up in the kitchen.

I empty the trash.

trash

I clean up in
the bathroom.
I wipe the counter.

counter

I clean up in
the bathroom.
I pick up the towels.

towels

Glossary

counter

spills

dishes

towels

Index

B

bed, 5

D

dishes, 14

S

spills, 10

T

trash, 18